Become a star reader

This three-level reading series is designe___
beginning readers and is based on popu___ ___ ___ episodes.
The books feature common sight words used with limited grammar.
Each book also offers a set number of target words. These words
are noted in bold print and are presented in a picture dictionary
in order to reinforce meaning and expand reading vocabulary.

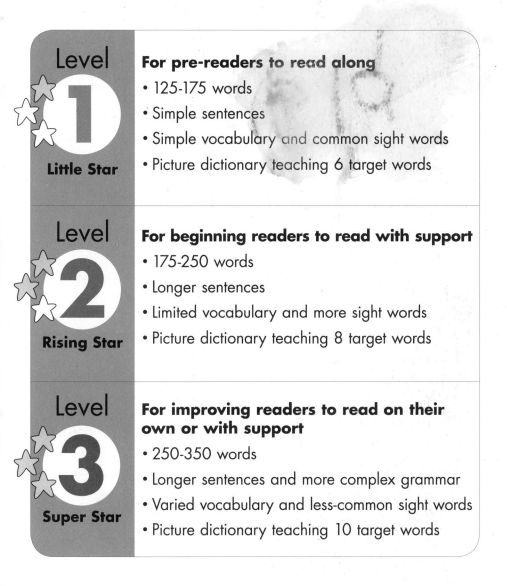

Level 1 — Little Star

For pre-readers to read along

- 125-175 words
- Simple sentences
- Simple vocabulary and common sight words
- Picture dictionary teaching 6 target words

Level 2 — Rising Star

For beginning readers to read with support

- 175-250 words
- Longer sentences
- Limited vocabulary and more sight words
- Picture dictionary teaching 8 target words

Level 3 — Super Star

For improving readers to read on their own or with support

- 250-350 words
- Longer sentences and more complex grammar
- Varied vocabulary and less-common sight words
- Picture dictionary teaching 10 target words

Text: adaptation by Rebecca Klevberg Moeller
All rights reserved.
Original story written by Marion Johnson, based on the animated series CAILLOU
Illustrations: Eric Sévigny, based on the animated series CAILLOU

The PBS KIDS logo is a registered mark of PBS and is used with permission.

Chouette Publishing would like to thank the Government of Canada and SODEC
for their financial support.

Bibliothèque et Archives nationales du Québec and Library and Archives
Canada cataloguing in publication

Moeller, Rebecca Klevberg
Caillou: circus fun
(I read with Caillou)
Adaptation of: Caillou: The circus parade.
For children aged 3 and up.

ISBN 978-2-89718-343-1

1. Caillou (Fictitious character) - Juvenile literature. 2. Circus - Juvenile
literature. I. Sévigny, Éric. II. Johnson, Marion, 1949-   . Circus parade. III.
Title. IV. Title: Circus fun.

GV1817.M63 2016   j791.3   C2016-940291-6

Printed in China
10 9 8 7 6 5 4 3 2 1   CHO1972 MAY2016

Circus Fun

Text: Rebecca Klevberg Moeller, Language Teaching Expert
Illustrations: Eric Sévigny, based on the animated series

Today Caillou and Daddy are going to the **circus**!

Caillou likes the **circus** very much.
He wants to be a lion tamer!

Caillou is up early. He can not sleep!

Caillou jumps out of bed and finds his clothes.

Caillou puts on his shirt and underwear. He puts on his socks and shoes.

Caillou is just about ready
for the **circus**!

First, Caillou must brush his teeth.
"Caillou, it's very early!" Daddy
says.

"Why are you brushing your teeth?" Caillou answers, "The **circus** is today, Daddy!"

"The **circus** is not today, Caillou. The **circus** is tomorrow."

Oh no! Caillou is very sad.
He wants to see the **clowns**!

Daddy has an idea. "Let's have a **circus** breakfast today!"

"Hooray!" Caillou says. "I want to **juggle** the **eggs**!"

Caillou gets the **eggs**. "Look out for Gilbert!"

Caillou, Gilbert and the **eggs** fall on the floor.

"Caillou, we do not **juggle eggs**!"
Daddy says. What a **mess**!

After that, Daddy makes toast. It is very hot! Daddy **juggles** the hot **toast**. It falls on the floor.

"Funny **juggling**, Daddy!" Caillou laughs.

"Now let's have a **circus parade**!" Daddy says.

He carries Rosie. She is the **clown**. She has a funny hat. It is a funny **parade**!

Daddy goes first. He sings **circus** songs. He **dances** with Rosie.

It is a funny singing and **dancing parade**!

Caillou plays the **music**. He plays a pot with a spoon.

Now it is a funny, singing,
dancing, music parade!

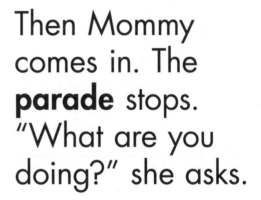

Then Mommy comes in. The **parade** stops. "What are you doing?" she asks.

"We are having a **circus parade**!" Daddy answers.

"It is a **noisy parade**!" says Mommy. "Please be quiet."

She looks around
the kitchen. "It is a
messy parade, too!
Please clean up."

Daddy and Caillou clean up the **mess**. The **circus parade** starts again.

It is a funny, singing, **dancing,
music parade**. But now it is
a quiet and clean **parade**, too!

Picture Dictionary

eggs **mess/messy**

circus **clown**

juggle/juggling **toast**

dance/dancing **parade**

noisy **music**